Heart Songs

By Christi Checkett

An Angel Playing a Flageolet by Edward Burne-Jones Public domain image.

Copyright © 2014 Christi Checkett

All rights reserved. No part of this book may be reproduced, stored in a retrieval system or transmitted in any form or by any means without the prior written permission of the publishers, except by a reviewer who may quote brief passages in a review to be printed in a newspaper, magazine or journal.

All images have been taken from public domain.

First printing

ISBN-13:978-1495440724

ISBN-10:1495440729

Legacy

St. Louis, MO

Printed in the United States of America

Available on Amazon.com

Introduction

You Can Trust Jesus. Jesus is the Word of God made flesh. He is the fulfillment of Old Testament law, Lord and King of all. After Jesus ascended to His Father, the Holy Spirit was sent to serve as our guide and comforter. The power of the Holy Spirit is the same power that raised Christ from the dead and now abides with believers today to guide them into all truth.

All you need to do is to turn your life over to Jesus. Simply ask Him to come and take the reigns of your heart and life. Have faith in Him and trust and believe that He is working all things for your ultimate good.

In Matthew 11: ^{Jesus said:} "Come to Me, all *you* who labor and are heavy laden, and I will give you rest. Take My yoke upon you and learn from Me, for I am gentle and lowly in heart, and you will find rest for your souls. For My yoke *is* easy and My burden is light."

If you are filled with fear and worry; turn your life over to Jesus. He will take the burden of your pain on to Himself and you will be set free to live according to your Heavenly Father's plan for your life. All you need to have is faith and believe that He hears your call. I promise you that you can turn your life over to Him knowing and trusting that His plans are what can be considered to be the best for your life.

Mark 11:22: ^(Jesus said,) "Have faith in God."

Once you have handed the reigns of your life over to Christ, it is now time to remain in a faith that can be defined as having complete belief, trust and confidence in God. Then, no matter the circumstances of your life, you will be at peace. Know that God has a good plan for your life and only He knows what is needed to put that plan into action. Then when you do not get the answer you want to a spoken prayer, at the time you want, you will be assured that God has something better for you.

This type of faith will give you the confidence to wait on Him, fully believing that God has the power to do whatever it is that you are asking . . . **IF** He feels it is in His best interest for you. Then, if the plan you had in mind changes, you can rely fully on the fact that something needed to change or God would not have made the change.

Who is Jesus?

Jesus is Lord and Savior to all who believe. He is food to your spirit and the light of the world. He is the gate to eternal salvation. All who pass through His gate will be safe and find pasture. Once you find Him, you live under the care of the one who laid down His life for you.

Those who believe will not die. He is the way. He is the truth, and He is the life. He is the only way to the Father and He is the vine that joins you to the vinedresser. You can find Him in both the Old and New Testament writings. Come to know Him better by feeding your spirit with the His Word.

Your journey with Christ begins with a simple prayer.
However, this simple prayer will change your entire life.

Salvation

One cold and dark grey winter's day,
With outstretched arms I cried and prayed
That Christ would take my sins away
And He, not I, the price would pay.

To ask was all I needed do.
And His great mercy did pour through.
Now with old flesh walks spirit new
To share God's love with you.

God the Father

^{Jesus said,} "This, then, is how you should pray: "'Our Father in heaven, hallowed be your name," Matthew 6:9 (NIV)

Jesus tells his disciples to believe that God is their Father. Believe His words, for you too have a Father in heaven caring deeply for you. You can trust Him. You can ask Him for whatever you need. You can ask for His will to come to your life, or for forgiveness. You can ask Him for things such as food or still better, deliverance from the temptation of the evil one.

Have faith that He hears your prayers. Jesus said, "When you pray, say: Our Father in heaven Hallowed be Your name. Your kingdom come Your will be done On earth as it is in heaven. Give us day by day our daily bread. And forgive us our sins, For we also forgive everyone who is indebted to us. And do not lead us into temptation, But deliver us from the evil one."

Although the blessing seems too vast for human comprehension, do not stagger at His promises in unbelief, for God tells us to ask, knock and seek:

"Ask, and it will be given to you; seek, and you will find; knock, and it will be opened to you. For everyone who asks receives, and he who seeks finds, and to him who knocks it will be opened. Or what man is there among you who, if his son asks for bread, will give him a stone? Or if he asks for a fish, will he give him a serpent? If you then, being evil, know how to give good gifts to your children, how much more will your Father who is in heaven give good things to those who ask Him!" (Matthew 7:7).

Did You Know That You Look Like Your Father?

The Bible tells us that God said, let us [Father, Son, and Holy Spirit] make mankind in Our image, after Our likeness (Genesis 1:26).

The one true all powerful and Almighty God is your Father. You are made in His image. That means you look like your Father! God is made up of three parts – Father, Son and Holy Spirit and you are made up of three parts. You have a body, soul and spirit.

Place your faith and trust in God – Your Father. Your Heavenly Father loves you. He is there to comfort you in times of sorrow or pain. You can be certain that when it is needed, that you will find comfort in your Father's arms.

Comfort in His Arms

Wherever there is sorrow,
Wherever there is scorn
Wherever there is hopelessness
There is comfort in God's arms.
For He's our heavenly Father,
With a heart of love so true,
To comfort and bring hope when pain
Sets out to destroy you.

He sits above the Heavens,
Yet dwells with those on earth
To find a heart that seeks to know
The power of rebirth.
A birth found in the Son of God,
Christ Jesus is His name.
He came to heal the broken heart,
The blind, the bruised, the lame.

He came to set you free once more,
From Satan, sin and death.
He came to give you faith and hope,
And love, joy, peace, and breath.
He came in order that you know

Your Father, up above.
He came that man might feel once more
The comfort of God's love.

Salvation comes the day we call
Upon God's only son.
Foundation's laid as God reveals
His true and risen one.

And thus our hearts are filled with praise
As we exalt Christ's name
To manifest and magnify
The reason why Christ came.

If you are seeking shelter
From Satan's fears and harm.
Place your faith in Jesus Christ.
He'll place you in God's arms.

There is comfort in His arms.

The Trinity

Father, you're the source of all
The wellspring of all things,

And Christ, in you all wisdom dwells,
You are the King of Kings.

Holy Spirit, how we need your power
Indwell us through and through,
And use us in this final hour
As we draw near to you.

Hubble Telescope Image – Public Domain

The Seen and Unseen Creation

I view my world
The stars, the skies, the seas,
As my God's handiwork,
Creation made for me.

In viewing it,
I fall upon my knees,
And thank you God
For all that I can see.

Yet lives another world,
One hid from view,
Created by my Father
for me too.
It guards and watches over
all I do
And for that world my Father
I thank you.

You set your angels, Father,
all around,
Though with my eyes,
Their forms cannot be found.
Yet they exist
As real as this earth's ground
To help me on the path
That's Heaven bound.

Lord, I would like to pause
And give you praise
For setting guards around me
all my days
And though my eyes are hid
from angels ways,
In thanks for them
. To you my voice is raised.

The Gardener

A vineyard planted long ago

Had a tree of figs

That would not grow.

The owner came and felt despair.

He sought out fruit

But none was there.

In sadness to his gardener said,

"We'll cut it down

It's better dead."

The gardener

In defense of tree,

Asked the responsibility

To dig and dung

So it would grow

And fruit he would the owner show.

The two agreed -

A new plan try.

If fruit grew not

The tree must die.

The Lord, the vineyard,

And the tree,

Bare messages

For you and me.

God in despair

Of vineyard's man

Bought to this world

A better plan.

His Son was sent

To dig and dung

As He upon the cross was hung.

And with His resurrection bought

The chance to grow the fruit God sought.

Now I can live eternally

Because the gardener died for me.

Abraham going up to offer Isaac as a sacrifice
Holman Bible – Public Domain

The Father's Sacrifice

Long ago
So long forgotten,
God said, "Abraham take heed.
Offer me thy son beloved.
Sacrifice thy only seed."

Three days journey to Moriah
On a mountain near the sky
Isaac lay upon an altar
Obediently prepared to die.

Abraham so loved the Father.
His beloved son he'd feely give.
God in seeing such devotion
Allowed Isaac, then, to live.

A beloved son – a beautiful offering
To our glorious God on high.
Our God would place His own beloved
Son in Satan's hands to die.

A beloved son – a Holy offering
And our gift from God above.
No retreat now, No retrieval,
For God gave His son with love.

Many years had passed in waiting
For this Calvary near the sky.
On a rugged cross our Savior
Hung obediently to die.

No retreat now, No retrieval,
God provides Himself a lamb.
Crushing Satan's hold on sinners
Long foretold by Abraham.

.

The True Bread of Life

My Lord, through your miracles
You showed all your Word.
They saw, and they listened.
But most never heard.

The reasons they followed
Are hard to believe
The sought not the wisdom
But food they could see.

The true bread of life
You patiently told
Cannot be bought
And cannot be sold.

Yet, those who receive it
Will no longer thirst,
And no longer hunger,
For the bread of this earth.

And all who are given
From Your Father to thee
Will hear, and will see,
And will truly believe

That the true bread of life
Is found in your blood
And found in your flesh
That you offered with love.

I thank you My Lord
For the true gift you gave.
It's food, and it's truth, and
It's my life you saved.

Christ Pantokrator, 6th Century, St. Catherine's Monastery

Read my Word.

Look and see
All the things
I ask of thee.
Believing first
My blood was shed
To pardon sin
And raise the dead,
Providing too
A plan for man
To walk in truth
And love again.
Read me daily,
Faithfully,
Gaining strength
And love for me
To arm yourself
So you can flee
From Satan's
Pain and misery.

Behold, a virgin shall be with child, and shall bring forth a son, and they shall call his name Emmanuel, which being interpreted is, God with us.

Matthew 1:23

Therefore the Lord himself will give you a sign: The virgin will conceive and give birth to a son, and will call him Immanuel.

Isaiah 7:14

The Birth of Jesus

When we say that Jesus Christ was born of a virgin, in reality, we are indicating what took place at His conception, not at the time of His birth. Christ had no human biological father. He was not conceived through the help of a man. He was conceived by God through the Holy Spirit. The gospel of Luke gives this beautiful account of the announcement of the virgin birth to Mary.

"Now in the sixth month the angel Gabriel was sent by God to a city of Galilee named Nazareth, to a virgin betrothed to a man whose name was Joseph, of the house of David. The virgin's name was Mary. And having come in, the angel said to her, "Rejoice, highly favored one, the Lord is with you; blessed are you among women!"

But when she saw him, she was troubled at his saying, and considered what manner of greeting this was. Then the angel said to her, "Do not be afraid, Mary, for you have found favor with God. And behold, you will conceive in your womb and bring forth a Son, and shall call His name JESUS. He will be great, and will be called the Son of the Highest; and the Lord God will give Him the throne of His father David. And He will reign over the house of Jacob forever, and of His kingdom there will be no end."

Mary said to the angel, "How can this be, since I do not know a man?"

And the angel answered and said to her, "The Holy Spirit will come upon you, and the power of the Highest will overshadow you; therefore, also, that Holy One who is to be born will be called the Son of God. Now indeed, Elizabeth your relative has also conceived a son in her old age; and this is now the sixth month for her who was called barren. For with God nothing will be impossible."

Then Mary said, "Behold the maidservant of the Lord! Let it be to me according to your word." And the angel departed from her. Luke 1:26-38

It is important to note in this scripture that "Gabriel was sent from God to a virgin betrothed [but not yet married] to a man whose name was Joseph, of the house of David. The two crucial facts here are that Mary was a virgin, and Joseph was of the house of David. Mary's virginity is important because it meant she was not pregnant already, thus telling us that a virgin conceived a child whose Father was God and not a man. It was also important that Joseph belonged to the house of David. Legally Joseph's relationship to Jesus put Jesus in the Davidic line. This enabled him to fulfill the promises made to in the Old Testament.

How can a virgin conceive? The angel told Mary that this is how it would happen.

"The Holy Spirit will come upon you and the power of the Most High will overshadow you, *THEREFORE* the child to be born will be called holy, the *SON OF GOD*."

I do not understand but I believe that is how it happened. The answer for me ultimately has to be what Gabriel said to Mary, "For with God nothing will be impossible."

Jesus can be called Son of God only because he was "conceived by the Holy Spirit, born of the Virgin Mary." It is important that you grasp that God was Jesus' Father. This signifies the union of God with man in Jesus Christ. Jesus could take on our humanity and full human nature while remaining fully God. He was Emanuel, God with us, coming to rescue a fallen world

God with Us

How precious is Thy name
Oh Jesus Christ – divine.
A virgin birthed this child conceived –
A king From David's line.

Born to remove all sins
And cleanse us from all stains
Until purity and love prevail
And only light remains.

In gratitude our King
Our lives we fully give
To serve and reign
With Christ our King
Forever we will live

The author of the gospel of Luke was a historian and a physician. Although he never met Jesus face to face, he often met with eye witnesses of Jesus and those who were with Christ from the beginning. It is believed that Luke attained much of the information for his gospel from Jesus' mother, Mary. Many feel that the gospel of Luke is written from Mary's point of view. I believe this to be true. Nothing could be more beautiful than Luke's description of the birth of Christ. The details of His birth were said to have been kept in Mary's heart all those years. They come to life in a way that only a mother could speak of the night her savior was born. I will give the account in its entirety.

Luke writes, "And it came to pass in those days that a decree went out from Caesar Augustus that all the world should be registered. This census first took place while Quirinius was governing Syria. So all went to be registered, everyone to his own city.

Joseph also went up from Galilee, out of the city of Nazareth, into Judea, to the city of David, which is called Bethlehem, because he was of the house and lineage of David, to be registered with Mary, his betrothed wife, who was with child. So it was, that while they were there, the days were completed for her to be delivered. And she brought forth her firstborn Son, and wrapped Him in swaddling clothes, and laid Him in a manger, because there was no room for them in the inn.

Now there were in the same country shepherds living out in the fields, keeping watch over their flock by night. And behold, an angel of the Lord stood before them, and the glory of the Lord shone around them, and they were greatly afraid. Then the angel said to them, "Do not be afraid, for behold, I bring you good tidings of great joy which will be to all people. For there is born to you this day in the city of David a Savior, who is Christ the Lord. And this will be the sign to you: You will find a Babe wrapped in swaddling clothes, lying in a manger."

And suddenly there was with the angel a multitude of the heavenly host praising God and saying: "Glory to God in the highest, And on earth peace, goodwill toward men!" So it was, when the angels had gone away from them into heaven, that the shepherds said to one another, "Let us now go to Bethlehem and see this thing that has come to pass, which the Lord has made known to us." And they came with haste and found Mary and Joseph, and the Babe lying in a manger. Now when they had seen Him, they made widely known the saying which was told them concerning this Child. And all those who heard it marveled at those things which were told them by the shepherds. But Mary kept all these things and pondered them in her heart.

The Birth of Jesus

A babe was born in Bethlehem
Quietly, so quietly.
The star shone bright to tell of Him
Joyfully, so joyfully.

For God possessed a saving plan
Eternally, unfailingly.
This babe would grow into a man
Faithfully, trustingly
Then place His fate in Father's hands
Willingly, forgivingly

Defeating Satan's rule of man.

The Death of Jesus

Scripture verse And when the centurion, who stood there in front of Jesus, saw how he died, he said, "Surely this man was the Son of God!" [**Mark 15:39**]

It is important to understand that Christ died that day He was crucified. He had expired prior to the sword penetrating His heart. Some would have you to believe that He was only partially dead, then taken somewhere to recuperate from his wounds. No, He was completely dead. Thus, only a power beyond human understanding could resurrect Him. That same power that raised Christ from the dead is alive within you this day. It is the Holy Spirit.

Joseph of Arimathea wrapped the body of Jesus in a piece of linen cloth and placed Him in a new tomb that was to be for him. John refers to strips of linen used for His burial, and Peter found multiple pieces of burial cloth after the tomb was found open. There were strips of linen cloth for the body and a separate cloth for the head. Some believe that these burial cloths can be seen today.

Although our faith cannot be confirmed or shaken by an artifact or anything else that can be seen with our eyes, it is interesting to study one of the burial cloths known as the Shroud of Turin. The shroud's most distinctive characteristic is the faint image of a front and back view of a naked man with his hands folded. The image has a beard, a moustache, and shoulder-length hair parted in the middle. He is muscular and tall for that time, approximately 5'7". The details of the image on the shroud are not easily seen by the naked eye.

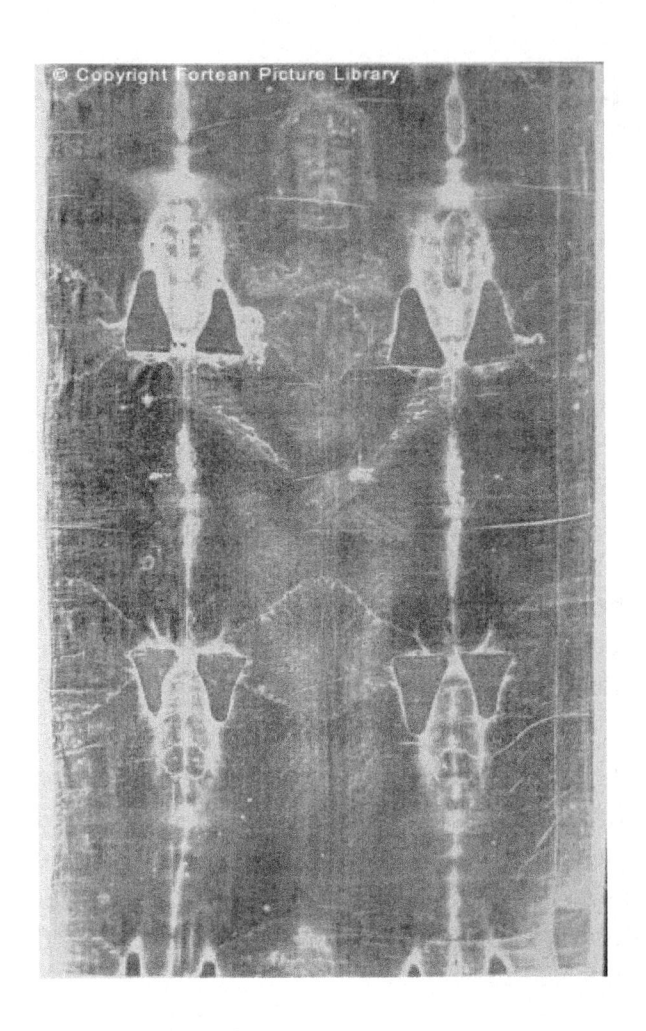

They were first noticed when photographs were taken of the image. In 1898 Secondo Pia took the first photograph of the shroud. He was startled in his darkroom when he saw the visible image on the negative plate. The negative of the Shroud gives the appearance of a positive image. This signifies that the shroud itself is a negative of some sort. Researchers concluded in 2011 that the shroud could not have been forged during the Middle Ages as once was the prevalent thought.

There are reddish brown blood stains on the cloth. The stains correlate with the Biblical description of the death Christ:

- one wrist bears a large, round wound, the second wrist is hidden by the folding of the hands
- an upward wound in the side penetrating the thoracic cavity with red blood cells and serum draining from the lesion
- small punctures around the forehead and scalp
- numerous wounds on the torso and legs consistent with the distinctive dumbbell wounds of a Roman flagrum.
- swelling of the face from severe beatings
- streams of blood down both arms, in response to gravity at an angle that would occur during crucifixion
- no evidence of either leg being fractured
- large puncture wounds in the feet as if pierced by a single spike

Pope John Paul II showed himself to be deeply moved when he viewed the image of the Shroud stating "The Shroud is an image of God's love as well as of human sin. The imprint left by the tortured body of the Crucified One, which attests to the tremendous human capacity for causing pain and death to one's fellow man, stands as an icon of the suffering of the innocent in every age." Christ bore the sins of the world that day on the cross. The innocent took the place of the guilty so the guilty could live.

Whether the cloth is authentic or not has no bearing whatsoever on the validity of what Jesus taught or on the saving power of his death and resurrection. Understand that faith is believing what cannot be seen.

Shroud of Turin - Public Domain

Man of Sorrows – Isaiah 53

Oh precious man of sorrows
Descended from on high
Despised, scorned, and rejected
You turned not from my cry.

Made lower than the angels
My Lord this had to be,
To conquer sin,
To conquer death,
You had to die for me.

Through your death
You bore my sin
Now I can be set free
And Jesus, deep inside I know
You'd do this just for me.

A seed you say will serve you,
To proclaim your mighty deed,
Displaying too your righteousness,
I want to be that seed.

Resurrection Sunday
[Mary Magdalene's Song]

It's early dawn
This quiet morn,
The first day of the week,
Rome just crucified my Lord.
It is Him I seek.
For often I would talk with Him
I learned the truths He'd say,
And often I would walk with Him,

I loved Him more each day.

He taught me how to really love.
He taught me how to pray.
Demons He cast out of me,
All seven sent away.
The stone's been moved.
They've taken Him.
I'm blinded by my tears.
A voice calls out,
"Whom seekest thou?"
And Jesus Christ appeared.

Then Mary felt the joy and peace
That only Christ can bring.
We too can share these precious gifts
When walking with our king.

Empty Tomb

Victorious Son

My Lord you are the crown of life
You destined us to reign.
Yet in the fall,
Man's fall from you
Your joy turned into pain.

To overcome the evil one's
The task that lies ahead.
The power came that precious day
That Christ rose from the dead.

For hell could not encompass Him
Our victory was won.
Eternally we'll praise the name
Of our God's holy Son

Hubble Telescope Image – Public Domain

Eternal King

I'll bow my knee
I'll bow my head
To serve my King
Raised from the dead.
A willing subject
I will be
Because my King
Has died for me.

Other kings
On earth will reign,
Command respect,
Receive acclaim.
Yet only one
The ransom paid
When His own life
In death He laid.

Now I can live eternally
Because my King has died for me.

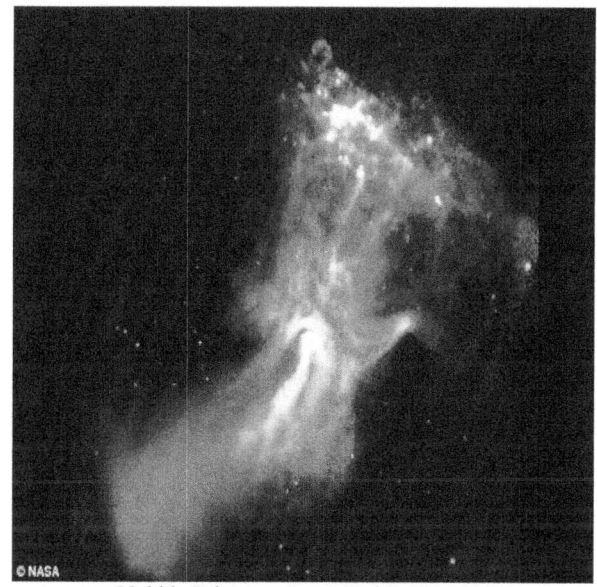

Hubble Telescope Image Public Domain

Praise

My Lord you are the source of life,
Creator all in all,
As heaven is, on earth, we'll see
Salvation from the Fall.

What joy! What peace!
What strength you bring.
Your kingdom God is nigh.
You are the Lord, The risen King,
On earth – land, sea and sky.

With every breath I'll praise your name
Through ages shining bright
As heaven is, make earth the same
Turn darkness into light

Prayer

Most holy one of Israel
Our hearts cry out to you.
Remove, oh Lord, our bondages
Cleanse our dark hearts too.

For you alone are God most high
You alone are king
In righteousness and truth you reign
You're Lord of everything.

Together now in one accord
Our voices shall ascend.
To praise the Bread of Life – The Word
Forever, without end.

Hubble Telescope Image Public Domain

Grace

I praise You
That it's You
And You alone.
Who picks us up,
And carries
Each one home.

May all our praises
Rise before
Your throne.
For making
Your own will
Our very own.
I give you thanks My God
I stand in awe
For in Your death
You saved us
From death's claws.

And even though
We're tarnished
And have flaws,
It's grace
By which we're saved
And not the law.

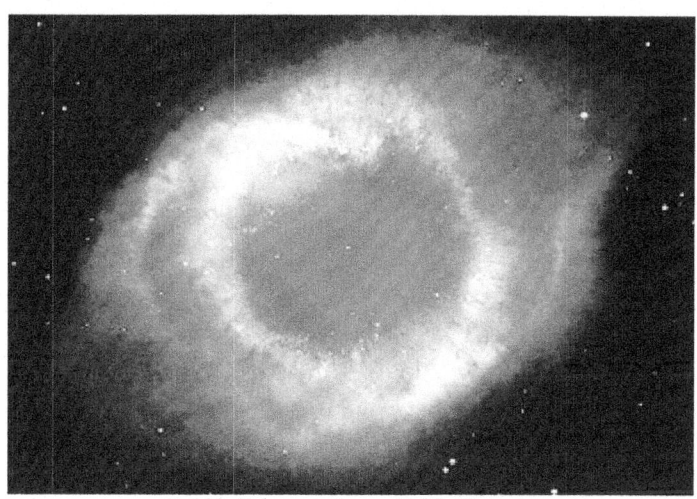

Hubble Telescope Image Public Domain

Justification

Undeserving, also humbled
Do I bow before your throne.
For I can come before you
Since Christ's righteousness
Is my own.

Guard me Lord,
And keep me,
As the Father keeps his own,
And guide me down
This path of life,
Until I am safely home.

The Holy Spirit

Jesus said, "When the Advocate comes, whom I will send to you from the Father — the Spirit of truth who goes out from the Father — he will testify about me" (John16:26).

Chapter 15 of John tells of Jesus making known to the disciples that He will be going away to His Father. First they hear the sad news but then the Lord tells them why this must happen. His words convey a beautiful expression of love and hope.

"But now I go away to Him who sent Me, and none of you asks Me, 'Where are You going?' But because I have said these things to you, sorrow has filled your heart. Nevertheless I tell you the truth. It is to your advantage that I go away; for if I do not go away, the Helper will not come to you; but if I depart, I will send Him to you. And when He has come, He will convict the world of sin, and of righteousness, and of judgment: of sin, because they do not believe in Me; of righteousness, because I go to My Father and you see Me no more; of judgment, because the ruler of this world is judged.

"I still have many things to say to you, but you cannot bear them now. However, when He, the Spirit of truth, has come, He will guide you into all truth; for He will not speak on His own authority, but whatever He hears He will speak; and He will tell you things to come. He will glorify Me, for He will take of what is Mine and declare it to you. All things that the Father has are Mine. Therefore I said that He will take of Mine and declare it to you.- A little while, and you will not see Me; and again a little while, and you will see Me, because I go to the Father" (John 16:5).

In this passage Jesus is telling the disciples that He is getting ready to go away. He knows that sorrow is filling their hearts. However, He is also letting them know that it will be to their advantage. This is because of the fact that the next thing that God wants to do cannot happen unless the last thing that He was doing comes to an end.

It is during these times that it looks like nothing is happening or you feel like God has gone away somewhere. He is still there and He is getting you ready for the next thing He wants to do. You need not be afraid for He is with you.

The Comforter

Fear no more,
My little child,
My Spirit dwells in you.
Unafraid and fearless walk
In all that you must do.

Proclaim my name where you talk
To all that you might meet.
Spread my peace where you walk
To everyone you greet.

Present yourself devotedly
To Jesus Christ the King.
Call others to His saving grace
With joy salvation brings.
For you are not alone my child,
Your companion dwells within,
Born to expose the devil's snares
And pardon man from sin.

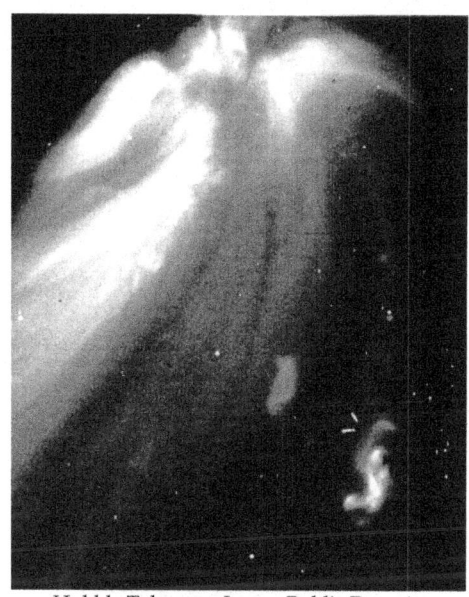

Hubble Telescope Image Public Domain

Glorification

Christ Jesus magnify yourself
Walk closely by my side.
In nothing may I shame you.
My dear Lord be my guide.

To live means only life through you.
To die would be my gain;
For I could gaze upon your face
Where peace and safety reign.

Yet something calls me back again
Your Word is needed here.
People are in bondage
They lie awake in fear.

Prepare me then to tell them
I'll study and I'll pray,
To walk sincere and blameless
So others walk your way.

Hubble Telescope Image Public Domain

The Gift

Lord I would like to say to you
There's nothing I could say or do
To merit such a gift.

You've known me from the very start
There's nothing in my mind or heart
To warrant such a gift.

But You in mercy gave to me
Your gift of life eternally
From death and sin
You set me free
I praise you for your gift.

So I would like to give to you
My heart and mind in all I do
And You will make me holy too
In giving me your gift.

Jesus Will Return

On that day his feet will stand on the Mount of Olives, east of Jerusalem, and the Mount of Olives will be split in two from east to west, forming a great valley. - Zechariah 14:4

"So when they had come together, they asked Him, "Lord, will You at this time restore the kingdom to Israel?" He said to them, "It is not for you to know times or seasons which The Father has fixed by His own authority. But you shall receive power when the Holy Spirit has come upon you; and you shall be My witnesses in Jerusalem and in all Judea and Samaria and to the end of the earth."

And when He had said this, as they were looking on, He was lifted up, and a cloud took Him out of their sight. And while they were gazing into heaven as He went, behold, two men stood by them in white robes, and said, "Men of Galilee, why do you stand looking into heaven? This Jesus, Who was taken up from you into heaven, will come in the same way as you saw Him go into heaven." Then they returned to Jerusalem from the mount called Olivet, which is near Jerusalem" (Acts 1:6-12).

Hubble Telescope Image Public Domain

Come Lord Jesus

The trees cry out to you
    Come Lord Jesus come.
And with them I cry too
    Come Lord Jesus come.

Now listen to the wind
Cry out among the trees
    Come Lord Jesus come.
And as you hear that sound
Please listen Lord to me
    Come Lord Jesus come.

And riding on the wind are
Sweet songs of the birds singing
    Come Lord Jesus come.
And lifted up to you
My voice can still be heard singing
    Come Lord Jesus come.

All Creation will cry out
    Come Lord Jesus come.
And with it I will shout
    Come Lord Jesus come.

My Prayer

Teach me how to trust in you
My Father

Teach me how to walk just like
Your Son

Holy Spirit,
Empty me, and then fill me.
Until God's work is done.

But my life is worth nothing to me unless I use it for finishing the work assigned me by the Lord Jesus—the work of telling others the Good News about the wonderful grace of God. **Acts 20:24 NLT**

Made in the USA
Coppell, TX
04 April 2020